I0475659

DO I REALLY NEED AN ATTORNEY?

CAN'T I JUST FILL IN THE BANKRUPTCY FORMS MYSELF?

(Including the 7 Most Common Bankruptcy Errors That Debtors Commit)

By Robert R. Goldstein,
Attorney at Law

Robert R. Goldstein
Attorney at Law
2734 East Main Street
Columbus, OH 43209
(614) 231-0003
www.goldsteinlawohio.com

Second Edition

ISBN: 978-1-304-74654-2

DISCLAIMER

The information given in this book is based upon the laws of the State of Ohio and generally pertains to practices of the Courts of Franklin County and/or the City of Columbus. The information is based on the law as it exists on January 1, 2014. The law is always subject to change and often changes to the law are made with little or no advance warning.

The information provided is both limited and general in nature. It is not meant to replace the advice of a competent attorney and should not be relied upon for any specific situation.

It is advised that you consult personally with an attorney of your choosing to discuss the details of your situation.

About The Author

Attorney Robert R. Goldstein was born and raised in Philadelphia, Pennsylvania. In 1983, Attorney Goldstein moved to Cleveland, Ohio, to attend Case Western Reserve University, where he served as Secretary of his fraternity, Zeta Beta Tau, and President of his class for his first two years of college. After earning his degree in Psychology, Attorney Goldstein worked a series of jobs ranging from computer consulting to selling fire extinguishers door-to-door, while he explored a career in stand-up comedy.

Two years later, having not successfully earned his own late night talk show, Attorney Goldstein decided to pursue a more stable career, so he began completing applications to enter a Masters' program in Social Work. During that process, he received a speeding ticket which changed his life forever. He defended himself in court, successfully obtaining a not guilty verdict, even though the police officer claimed to have caught him speeding with radar. Of the eight cases heard that day, only Mr. Goldstein was not found guilty. Attorney Goldstein immediately knew what needed to be done next.

In 1989, Attorney Goldstein moved to Columbus to attend The Ohio State University College of Law. He served as President of the Student Bar Association, receiving the coveted Bronze Key Award from the Law School Division of the American Bar Association. He earned his Juris Doctorate degree in law in 1992.

After passing the Ohio Bar Exam on his first attempt, Attorney Goldstein joined the Columbus office of the firm of Hyatt Legal Services, where he worked as a lawyer for three successful years, earning himself a promotion to the position of managing attorney. On September 15, 1995, Attorney Goldstein discovered that in starting his own Columbus based practice, he could be more effective in helping people deal with a variety of legal issues, including but not limited to Bankruptcy, Divorce, Dissolution, Civil, Criminal, Probate and Estate Planning matters. Since then, Attorney Goldstein has represented thousands of clients in State and Federal Courts throughout the Columbus area. Over the past 21 years, Attorney Goldstein has come to fully realize his passion for helping people at all levels of litigation in the Columbus area

Attorney Goldstein's non-legal interests continue to include magic, improv, and stand-up comedy, and he has performed in clubs and colleges all over the United States. He also spent many years in Columbus community theater and was a co-founder of the Columbus Lawyer's Performance Ensemble. His acting skills have been utilized in educational seminars for students, workshops for court security personnel and for lawyers' continuing legal education classes. His office in Bexley, Ohio services clients in the entire greater Columbus area

We are a debt relief agency. We help people file for Bankruptcy under the Bankruptcy Code.

INTRODUCTION

I have been practicing law for over twenty years. During that time, I have had the pleasure of meeting with over ten thousand potential clients. (Of course, not all of them have hired me.) I have been asked all types of questions about all types of things, but there is one question that I've heard more than any other. Almost once a week someone will ask me if they really need an attorney or can they just do it by their self. My answer is always the same.

"No. You don't need an attorney," I always say. Then I continue, "You don't need a mechanic to fix your car either, if you know how. You don't need a doctor to take out your appendix, either." We hire professionals to do things for us because they can usually do them better and more efficiently. The legal practice is no different.

Twenty five years ago, nobody would even think of going near a courthouse without bringing an attorney. What has changed in our society to make so many people think that lawyers are not necessary?

I believe that there are several factors. I don't know that any single factor alone would have caused such a revolution in people's thinking, but when all these factors combine, the result is certainly understandable.

First, just about the time I started law school, in the late 1980's, the legal community decided it was time for lawyers to stop using "legalese" and to start speaking English. There was a true and legitimate concern that clients did not understand essential aspects of their cases. Contracts which had previously used terms like "the party of the first part" and "the party of the second part" began simply using names of the parties. Terms like *per capita* and *per stirpes* were replaced by terms like "divide equally" and "to their descendants." Documents became clearer, more straightforward, and much easier to understand. While this was a huge step forward for clients, it meant that a law degree was no longer necessary to be able to read a legal document.

Around the same time, computer technology began to increase significantly and the use of the internet began to explode. Unbelievable amounts of information became readily available to the general public at very low or no costs. The magic and mystery of what happened in court rooms became totally exposed and clients were no longer in the dark regarding any aspect of their case.

Finally, this time period also saw an incredible increase in the number of people who decided to go to law school. According to Family Lawyer Magazine, in 1968 there were 168,000 licensed practicing attorneys. By 1980, the number had grown to 680,000. As of 2012, there were approximately 1.25 million attorneys in practice.

In the United States, 44,000 law students graduate each year. Ohio currently has nine accredited law schools. Several of those schools have both a day program and a night program. In 2013, 1,321 people passed the Ohio Bar Exam, making them eligible to practice law. While I don't know the exact statistics, I can only assume that less than a quarter of that number either passed away or retired. The State is becoming saturated with attorneys. Competition has forced many attorneys to offer ridiculously low fees. As attorneys in general devalue their worth, the public's opinion of the profession is also devalued proportionately.

Also, with such a large number of attorneys in practice, it is only logical that some will be less thorough and less professional than others. Their attention to detail may be less than noteworthy, which leads their clients to believe that the cases require minimal effort.

It is therefore not surprising to me that a large portion of the population believes that attorneys are not necessary for what appears to be simple straight forward tasks.

Unfortunately, they are wrong.

Error #1 - Looks Can Be Deceiving

One problem with the theory that attorneys are no longer necessary is that looks can be deceiving. While many legal tasks appear to be a matter of simply filling in the blanks, this assumes that all cases are the same. This is simply not true. Often, there are many nuances which must be considered, especially in bankruptcy.

Language is often a funny thing. If you don't ask the right question, you don't get the right answer. For the first few years of my practice, I would consistently ask people if they owned any real estate and I would consistently be told no, only to learn later that the client had owned a home for several years. When I inquired further they would always explain that they don't own their home, the bank owns it. Now I ask the client, "Are you currently *buying* any real estate?"

In the above example, the client thought he or she was being completely honest when he or she told me that he or she did not own any real estate. Unfortunately, had the information not been properly disclosed in the bankruptcy petition, the Judge would likely have found that perjury had occurred. When someone chooses not to use an attorney, he or she is still held to the same standards of practice as if an attorney had been involved.

The problem with just filling in forms is that you can only properly answer a question if you know exactly what the question is asking. While you can easily buy blank bankruptcy petitions, if you don't know what information is actually required in each schedule, then you can't competently fill in the blanks.

It is important to remember that bankruptcy petitions are signed under oath. All information is subject to examination by the Attorney General. Any person who makes a false oath or statement under penalty of perjury in connection with a bankruptcy case is subject to fine, imprisonment, or both.

Another important job of a bankruptcy attorney is to help the client rack his or her brain to be certain that no important information is omitted from the petition.

Questions like "have you been in a car accident in the past four years" or "does anybody owe you any money at all for any reason" can be invaluable in helping people not to forget to disclose important information. Someone who simply reads forms and tries to fill in blanks may not be triggered to remember everything and could suffer serious consequences as a result.

Error #2 – Forms Don't Tell You the Law

Another problem with someone trying to avoid an attorney and simply filling in the forms, is that the forms don't tell you the law. For example, the Bankruptcy Petition Schedule B, line 18 asks you to list "other liquidated debts owed to debtor including tax refunds." It does not inform you that if you are expecting a large tax refund at the time you file, the bankruptcy trustee can actually take that refund and use it to pay some of your bills. The form also does not tell you that the amount of your refund is pro-rated based on when you file. Someone who files his or her bankruptcy petition in January will be in a very different situation than someone who files a petition in June or in December. There are certain strategies which must be employed depending on each individual situation.

While there is plenty of information available through the internet as to obtaining forms and filling them out, there is virtually no free information to teach you strategy and how to avoid pit-falls. Quite simply, there is nothing which can replace the advice of a competent attorney, tailored to your individual needs.

Error #3 – The Law Is Always Changing

Although there haven't been any major bankruptcy changes since the Bankruptcy Abuse Prevention and Consumer Protection Act of 2005. Congress is still constantly making minor tweaks and changes to the laws and the forms. On December 1, 2013, changes were made to seven different official forms. On that same date, changes were made to six of the Rules of Bankruptcy Procedure.

Usually, the changes are very minor and sometimes they are merely changes in the style and appearance of the forms and have no impact on the content of the forms. As a result, the changes receive no media attention and are often not known to anyone who doesn't regularly file bankruptcy petitions or subscribe to a software maintenance program which will update the forms as changes are put into effect.

Nevertheless, the Bankruptcy Clerk of Courts will routinely reject any older form which has a newer counterpart. Sometimes the Court will give you an opportunity to amend the form and substitute a newer version for the one which was erroneously filed. However, the Court can deem the filing to be invalid and simply not acceptable. Depending on where you are in the process, you could forfeit court costs which are generally non-refundable.

Error #4 – Timing is Everything

Earlier I mentioned that there are strategies involved with when to file. This is true on several different levels.

One of the major changes made in 2005 relates to the time which must elapse between repeat filings. Technically, bankruptcy law does not set any minimum time that you need to wait before you can file for bankruptcy again. However, there is a catch. If you file too soon after you have received a discharge of your debts in a prior case, you cannot receive another discharge. Since this generally makes the second bankruptcy filing a waste of time and money, it is important to know the time frames that apply to receiving a second discharge.

The rules differ between Chapter 7 filings and Chapter 13 filings. It also matters the order in which you file. The rules are different if you file a Chapter 7 first and then want to file a Chapter 13 than if you file a Chapter 13 first and then later want to file a Chapter 7.

Sometimes a case is dismissed without a discharge being granted. In some cases, a new Petition can be immediately re-filed without any serious consequences. In other situations, it is necessary to wait a full year before re-filing, in order to maximize the benefits of the bankruptcy law.

Only an experienced attorney can properly analyze the rules and advise you of the best time to file. Utilizing the services of a non-attorney bankruptcy preparer or trying to download forms and fill them in yourself will not properly prepare you for potentially un-fixable problems.

Error #5 – Failure to Properly Communicate

In the Southern District of Ohio, which includes
Columbus, Cincinnati, and the surrounding areas, Local
Bankruptcy Rule 4002-1 requires debtors to bring 16
different items to the meeting of creditors hearing. Most
trustees require that some of those items be sent via fax or e-
mail prior to the hearing so they can be properly reviewed.

The trustees tend to be very unforgiving if
documentation is not transmitted at the proper time and in
the proper manner. At a minimum, most trustees will
immediately continue the hearing and the debtor will be
forced to come back to court again at a later date. Some
trustees will file a motion to dismiss the case and a
bankruptcy discharge will not be granted.

The bankruptcy trustees generally have a pretty
heavy caseload and they do not get paid enough to try to
help unrepresented debtors navigate the system. They
therefore tend to not be so patient to debtors who do not
properly follow all of the rules.

Again, without the help of an experienced attorney,
most people don't even know where to look to find the
rules. Bankruptcy practice is a combination of federal

statutes, federal rules of procedure, local rules of procedure, and case law. All of these sources must be properly synthesized in order to know what must be done in any given case.

Error #6 – Improper Estate Planning

By definition, bankruptcy means that your debts exceed your assets. If you could sell all of your property to pay your debts, there would be no reason to file bankruptcy.

Fortunately, the law also provides exemptions. Property which is exempt is therefore not included in the above equation. For example, in Ohio, you could claim an exemption in your motor vehicle for up to $3,675.00. This means that if you have equity in your vehicle for less than that amount then the court will not make you sell it.

Currently, the cash exemption is only $450.00. Therefore, if you have more than that amount on the day you file bankruptcy (which includes money owed to you, i.e. a tax refund) the Court could order you to surrender that money to the trustee for the benefit of your creditors.

A good bankruptcy attorney could counsel you on "estate planning" so that your excess cash could be converted into exempt items. This way you maximize your benefits by spending the cash on items which don't need to be surrendered. If you simply try to give the money away or hide it, you could be subjected to some very serious consequences. However, "estate planning" is perfectly legal and will protect any assets which you have, while still giving you all of the benefits of the bankruptcy.

Error #7 – Failure To Properly Prepare

To their credit, most of my bankruptcy clients have tried everything possible to avoid having to file bankruptcy. Unfortunately, this usually means that they have wasted a lot of money which could have been better used to pay for the filing or to help rebuild their lives after the bankruptcy is complete.

I have seen far too many clients attempt to avoid bankruptcy by rolling credit card balances from one card to another (known as kiting) or by taking out second mortgages to consolidate credit card debt. These practices can sometimes cause debts to become non-dischargeable and hurt the bankruptcy process.

Another dangerous mistake is when people try to pay back their family or friends so that they don't have to include those people in their bankruptcy. This is known as a "preference" and can have very undesired effects if proper bankruptcy strategy is not employed.

Part of the bankruptcy review includes actions which were taken prior to filing. In some cases, the court can look back as far as four years to determine whether or not a fraudulent transfer has occurred.

If you are even remotely thinking about bankruptcy, you would be well advised to meet with an attorney as soon as possible to discuss your options and how you should be acting to best remedy your financial situation.

Finally, The Good News

Finally, I have some good news for you. If you choose the right attorney, filing bankruptcy does not have to be so complicated and is not such a major ordeal.

A good attorney will thoroughly review you financial situation with you to determine your best course of action. In some cases, bankruptcy may not be necessary and debt negotiations may be a better course of action. In some cases, it might be best to file a Chapter 7 bankruptcy and eliminate all of your outstanding unsecured debt (with some exceptions, i.e. taxes, student loans, drunk driving injuries, etc.) In other cases, it might be best to file a Chapter 13 and reorganize your debt so that it can be satisfied over a period of time, usually with no interest paid. Only a skilled attorney can properly advise you on what works best for your situation.

When your bankruptcy is filed correctly and all appropriate deadlines are met, you can usually rest assured that discharge will be granted without any problems. (Of course, if there are unusual circumstances, then your attorney should explain those issues prior to filing and your attorney should be ready to defend any objections which may be raised or any motions which may be filed. It is absolutely imperative that you be completely open and honest with the attorney at the initial consultation so that no surprises occur during your case which could have otherwise been avoided.)

When evaluating a potential bankruptcy attorney, make sure that he or she has adequate experience and is knowledgeable about the current status of the law. (As an aside, I have represented clients in over 1,000 different cases. I have litigated issues with both creditors and trustees. I recently won a case against the U.S. Trustee's office over the dischargeability of debts which had been listed on a prior case which the client had filed without an attorney. The victory saved my client about $17,000.00)

With the right attorney, you can successfully rebuild your life financially, and start enjoying all that life has to offer. Every day you wait is one more day that your creditors prevent you from enjoying. Take control of your life today by calling an attorney to review your financial options. (As an aside, I can be reached at 614-231-0003 or through my website at www.goldsteinlawohio.com.)

Appendix - Disclosures

The law requires that certain disclosures be provided to all clients who receive bankruptcy advice from an attorney. While I have already provided a disclaimer that this book should not replace the advice of an attorney, I am including the necessary disclosure information for your review.

DISCLOSURE # 1

IMPORTANT INFORMATION ABOUT BANKRUPTCY AND ALTERNATIVES TO BANKRUPTCY PURSUANT TO 11 U.S.C. § 527(b)

IMPORTANT INFORMATION ABOUT BANKRUPTCY ASSISTANCE SERVICES FROM AN ATTORNEY OR BANKRUPTCY PETITION PREPARER

If you decide to seek bankruptcy relief, you can represent yourself, you can hire an attorney to represent you, or you can get help in some localities from a bankruptcy petition preparer who is not an attorney.

THE LAW REQUIRES AN ATTORNEY OR BANKRUPTCY PETITION PREPARER TO GIVE YOU A WRITTEN CONTRACT SPECIFYING WHAT THE ATTORNEY OR BANKRUPTCY PETITION PREPARER WILL DO FOR YOU AND HOW MUCH IT WILL COST.

1. Ask to see the contract before you hire anyone. The following information helps you understand what must be done in a routine bankruptcy case to help you evaluate how much service you need. Although bankruptcy can be complex, many cases are routine.

2. Before filing a bankruptcy case, either you or your attorney should analyze your eligibility for different forms of debt relief available under the Bankruptcy Code and which form of relief is most likely to be beneficial for you. Be sure you understand the relief you can obtain and its limitations.

3. To file a bankruptcy case, documents called a Petition, Schedules and Statement of Financial Affairs, as well as in some cases a Statement of Intention need to be prepared correctly and filed with the bankruptcy court. You will have to pay a filing fee to the bankruptcy court. Once your case starts, you will have to attend the required first meeting of creditors where you may be questioned by a court official called a 'trustee' and by creditors.

4. If you choose to file a chapter 7 case, you may be asked by a creditor to reaffirm a debt. You may want help deciding whether to do so. A creditor is not permitted to coerce you into reaffirming your debts.

5. If you choose to file a chapter 13 case in which you repay your creditors what you can afford over 3 to 5 years, you may also want help with preparing your chapter 13 plan and with the confirmation hearing on your plan which will be before a bankruptcy judge.

6. If you select another type of relief under the Bankruptcy Code other than chapter 7 or chapter 13, you will want to find out what should be done from someone familiar with that type of relief.

7. Your bankruptcy case may also involve litigation. You are generally permitted to represent yourself in litigation in

bankruptcy court, but only attorneys, not bankruptcy petition preparers, can give you legal advice.

DISCLOSURE # 2

PURPOSES, BENEFITS AND COSTS OF BANKRUPTCY PURSUANT TO CODE § 527(a)(1) & § 342(b)(1)

OFFICIAL FORM B 201 (04/09/06)

UNITED STATES BANKRUPTCY COURT
NOTICE TO INDIVIDUAL CONSUMER DEBTOR
UNDER § 342(b) OF THE BANKRUPTCY CODE

In accordance with § 342(b) of the Bankruptcy Code, this notice: (1) Describes briefly the services available from credit counseling services; (2) Describes briefly the purposes, benefits and costs of the four types of bankruptcy proceedings you may commence; and (3) Informs you about bankruptcy crimes and notifies you that the Attorney General may examine all information you supply in connection with a bankruptcy case. You are cautioned that bankruptcy law is complicated and not easily described. Thus, you may wish to seek the advice of an attorney to learn of your rights and responsibilities should you decide to file a petition. Court employees cannot give you legal advice.

1. Services Available from Credit Counseling Agencies

With limited exceptions, § 109(h) of the Bankruptcy Code requires that all individual debtors who file for bankruptcy relief on or after October 17, 2005, receive a briefing that outlines the available opportunities for credit counseling and provides assistance in performing a budget analysis.

The briefing must be given within 180 days before the bankruptcy filing. The briefing may be provided individually or in a group (including briefings conducted by telephone or on the Internet) and must be provided by a nonprofit budget and credit counseling agency approved by the United States trustee or bankruptcy administrator. The clerk of the bankruptcy court has a list that you may consult of the approved budget and credit counseling agencies.

In addition, after filing a bankruptcy case, an individual debtor generally must complete a financial management instructional course before he or she can receive a discharge. The clerk also has a list of approved financial management instructional courses.

2. The Four Chapters of the Bankruptcy Code Available to Individual Consumer Debtors Chapter 7: Liquidation ($245 filing fee, $46 administrative fee, $15 trustee surcharge: Total fee $306)

1. Chapter 7 is designed for debtors in financial difficulty who do not have the ability to pay their existing debts. Debtors whose debts are primarily consumer debts are subject to a "means test" designed to determine whether the case should be permitted to proceed under chapter 7. If your income is greater than the median income for your state of residence and family size, in some cases, creditors have the right to file a motion requesting that the court dismiss your case under § 707(b) of the Code. It is up to the court to decide whether the case should be dismissed.

2. Under chapter 7, you may claim certain of your property as exempt under governing law. A trustee may have the right to take possession of and sell the remaining property

that is not exempt and use the sale proceeds to pay your creditors.

3. The purpose of filing a chapter 7 case is to obtain a discharge of your existing debts. If, however, you are found to have committed certain kinds of improper conduct described in the Bankruptcy Code, the court may deny your discharge and, if it does, the purpose for which you filed the bankruptcy petition will be defeated.

4. Even if you receive a general discharge, some particular debts are not discharged under the law. Therefore, you may still be responsible for most taxes and student loans; debts incurred to pay nondischargeable taxes; domestic support and property settlement obligations; most fines, penalties, forfeitures, and criminal restitution obligations; certain debts which are not properly listed in your bankruptcy papers; and debts for death or personal injury caused by operating a motor vehicle, vessel, or aircraft while intoxicated from alcohol or drugs. Also, if a creditor can prove that a debt arose from fraud, breach of fiduciary duty, or theft, or from a willful and malicious injury, the bankruptcy court may determine that the debt is not discharged.

Chapter 13: Repayment of All or Part of the Debts of an Individual with Regular Income ($235 filing fee, $46 administrative fee: Total fee $281)

1. Chapter 13 is designed for individuals with regular income who would like to pay all or part of their debts in installments over a period of time. You are only eligible for chapter 13 if your debts do not exceed certain dollar amounts set forth in the Bankruptcy Code.

2. Under chapter 13, you must file with the court a plan to repay your creditors all or part of the money that you owe

them, using your future earnings. The period allowed by the court to repay your debts may be three years or five years, depending upon your income and other factors. The court must approve your plan before it can take effect.

3. After completing the payments under your plan, your debts are generally discharged except for domestic support obligations; most student loans; certain taxes; most criminal fines and restitution obligations; certain debts which are not properly listed in your bankruptcy papers; certain debts for acts that caused death or personal injury; and certain long term secured obligations.

Chapter 11: Reorganization ($1000 filing fee, $46 administrative fee: Total fee $1046)

Chapter 11 is designed for the reorganization of a business but is also available to consumer debtors. Its provisions are quite complicated, and any decision by an individual to file a chapter 11 petition should be reviewed with an attorney.

Chapter 12: Family Farmer or Fisherman ($200 filing fee, $46 administrative fee: Total fee $246)

Chapter 12 is designed to permit family farmers and fishermen to repay their debts over a period of time from future earnings and is similar to chapter 13. The eligibility requirements are restrictive, limiting its use to those whose income arises primarily from a family-owned farm or commercial fishing operation.

3. Bankruptcy Crimes and Availability of Bankruptcy Papers to Law Enforcement Officials

A person who knowingly and fraudulently conceals assets or makes a false oath or statement under penalty of perjury, either orally or in writing, in connection with a bankruptcy case is subject to a fine, imprisonment, or both. All information supplied by a debtor in connection with a bankruptcy case is subject to examination by the Attorney General acting through the Office of the United States Trustee, the Office of the United States Attorney, and other components and employees of the Department of Justice.

WARNING: Section 521(a)(1) of the Bankruptcy Code requires that you promptly file detailed information regarding your creditors, assets, liabilities, income, expenses and general financial condition. Your bankruptcy case may be dismissed if this information is not filed with the court within the time deadlines set by the Bankruptcy Code, the Bankruptcy Rules, and the local rules of the court.

Certificate of [Non-Attorney] Bankruptcy Petition Preparer

I, the [non-attorney] bankruptcy petition preparer signing the debtor's petition, hereby certify that I delivered to the debtor this notice required by § 342(b) of the Bankruptcy Code.

_____

Printed name and title, if any, of Bankruptcy Petition Preparer Social Security number (If the bankruptcy petition preparer is not an individual, state the Social Security Address: number of the officer, principal, responsible person, or _____
partner of the bankruptcy petition preparer.) (Required by 11 U.S.C. § 110.)

X_____

Signature of Bankruptcy Petition Preparer or officer, principal, responsible person, or partner whose Social Security number is provided above.

Certificate of the Debtor

I (We), the debtor(s), affirm that I (we) have received and read this notice.

_____   X_____
Printed Name(s) of Debtor(s)   Signature of Debtor

Date: _____ Case No. (if known)_____

X_____   _____
Signature of Joint Debtor (if any)   Date

The United States Constitution provides a method whereby individuals, burdened by excessive debt, can obtain a fresh financial start and pursue newly productive lives unimpaired by past financial problems. It is an important alternative for persons mired deep in financial difficulty.

The federal bankruptcy laws were enacted to provide debtors with a fresh start and to establish a ranking and equity among all the creditors who are clamoring for the debtor's limited resources. Bankruptcy helps people avoid the kind of permanent discouragement that can prevent them from ever reestablishing themselves as hard-working members of society. Also, creditors are ranked so that the debtor's nonexempt property can be fairly distributed according to established rules guaranteeing identical treatment to all creditors of the same rank.
This discussion is intended only as a brief overview of the types of bankruptcy filings and of what a bankruptcy filing

can and cannot do. Anyone considering this course of action is encouraged to seek the advice and assistance of an attorney specializing in bankruptcy law.

Types of Bankruptcy

The Bankruptcy Code is divided into chapters. The chapters which usually apply to consumer debtors are chapter 7, known as a Liquidation, and chapter 13, known as an Adjustment of the Debts of an Individual with Regular Income.

An important feature applicable to all types of bankruptcy filings is the automatic stay. The automatic stay means that the mere request for bankruptcy protection automatically "stays" or forces an abrupt halt to repossessions, foreclosures, evictions, garnishments, attachments, utility shut-offs, and debt collection harassment. It offers debtors a breathing spell by giving the debtor and the trustee assigned to the case time to review the situation and develop an appropriate plan. Creditors cannot take any further action against the debtor or the property without permission from the bankruptcy court.

Chapter 7

In a chapter 7, or liquidation case, the bankruptcy court appoints a trustee to examine the debtor's assets and divide them into exempt and nonexempt property. Exempt property is limited to a certain amount of equity in the debtor's residence, motor vehicle, household goods, life insurance, health aids, specified future earnings such as social security benefits and alimony, and certain other personal property. The trustee may then sell the nonexempt property and distribute the proceeds among the unsecured creditors. Although a liquidation case can rarely help with secured debt (the secured creditor still has the right to repossess the collateral), the debtor will be discharged from the legal obligation to pay unsecured debts such as credit card debts, medical bills and utility arrearages. However, certain types of unsecured debt are allowed special treatment and cannot be discharged. These include some student loans, alimony, child support, criminal fines, and some taxes.

Chapter 13

In a chapter 13 case, the debtor puts forward a plan, following the rules set forth in the bankruptcy laws, to repay all creditors over a period of time, usually from future income. A chapter 13 case may be advantageous in that the debtor is allowed to get caught up on mortgages or car loans without the threat of foreclosure or repossession and is allowed to keep both exempt and nonexempt property. The debtor's plan is a simple document outlining to the bankruptcy court how the debtor proposes to pay current expenses while paying off all the old debt balances. The debtor's property is protected from seizure from creditors, including mortgage and other lien holders, as long as the proposed payments are made. The plan generally requires monthly payments to the bankruptcy trustee over a period of three to five years. Arrangements can be made to have these payments made automatically through payroll deductions.

Chapter 11
(Taken from the official Public Information Series Bankruptcy Judges Division brochure on "Bankruptcy Basics" prepared by the Administrative Office of the United States Courts, June 2000)

A case filed under chapter 11 of the United States Bankruptcy Code is frequently referred to as a "reorganization" bankruptcy.

Upon the filing of a voluntary petition for relief under chapter the debtor automatically assumes an additional identity as the "debtor in possession."

The term refers to a debtor that keeps possession and control of its assets while undergoing a reorganization under chapter 11, without the appointment of a case trustee. A debtor will remain a debtor in possession until the debtor's plan of reorganization is confirmed, the debtor's case is dismissed or converted to chapter 7, or a chapter 11 trustee is appointed. The appointment or election of a trustee occurs only in a small number of cases. Generally, the debtor, as "debtor in possession," operates the business and performs many of the functions that a trustee performs in cases under other chapters. 11 U.S.C. § 1107(a). A written disclosure statement and a plan of reorganization must be filed with the court. 11 U.S.C. § 1121.

The disclosure statement is a document that must contain information concerning the assets, liabilities, and business affairs of the debtor sufficient to enable a creditor to make an informed judgment about the debtor's plan of reorganization. 11 U.S.C. § 1125. The information required is governed by judicial discretion and the circumstances of the case. The contents of the plan must include a classification of claims and must specify how each class of claims will be treated under the plan. 11 U.S.C. § 1123. Creditors whose claims are "impaired," i.e., those whose contractual rights are to be modified or who will be paid less than the full value of their claims under the plan vote on the plan by ballot. 11 U.S.C. § 1126. After the disclosure statement is approved and the ballots are collected and tallied, the bankruptcy court will conduct a confirmation hearing to determine whether to confirm the plan. 11 U.S.C. § 1128.

THE CHAPTER 11 DEBTOR –IN-POSSESSION

While individuals are not precluded from using chapter 11, it is more typically used to reorganize a business, which may be a corporation, sole proprietorship, or partnership. A corporation exists separate and apart from its owners, the stockholders. The chapter 11 bankruptcy case of a corporation (corporation as debtor) does not put the personal assets of the stockholders at risk other than the value of their investment in the company's stock.

A sole proprietorship (owner as debtor), on the other hand, does not have an identity separate and distinct from its owner(s); accordingly, a bankruptcy case involving a sole proprietorship includes both the business and personal assets of the owners-debtors. Like a corporation, a partnership exists separate and apart from its partners. In a partnership bankruptcy case (partnership as debtor), however, the partners' personal assets may, in some cases, be used to pay creditors in the bankruptcy case or the partners may, themselves, be forced to file for bankruptcy protection. Section 1107 of the Code places the debtor in possession in the position of a fiduciary, with the rights and powers of a chapter 11 trustee, and requires the performance of all but the investigative functions and duties of a trustee. These duties are set forth in the Bankruptcy Code and Federal Rules of Bankruptcy Procedure. 11 U.S.C. §§ 1106, 1107; Fed. R. Bankr. P. 2015(a). Such powers and duties include accounting for property, examining and objecting to claims, and filing informational reports as required by the court and the United States trustee, such as monthly operating reports. The debtor in possession also has many of the other powers and duties of a trustee including the right, with the court's approval, to employ attorneys, accountants, appraisers, auctioneers, or other professional persons to assist the debtor during its bankruptcy case.

Other responsibilities include filing tax returns and filing such reports as are necessary or as the court orders after confirmation, such as a final accounting. The United States trustee is responsible for monitoring the compliance of the debtor in possession with the reporting requirements. in a small business case. 11 U.S.C. § 1102(a)(3). A small business case proceeds faster than a regular chapter 11 case because the court may conditionally approve a disclosure statement, subject to final approval after notice and a hearing and solicitation of votes for acceptance or rejection of the plan. Thereafter, the disclosure statement hearing may be combined with the confirmation hearing.11 U.S.C. § 1125(f). In addition, the debtor has a shortened period of time (100 days from the date of the order for relief) within which only the debtor may file a plan.

Chapter 12
(Taken from the official Public Information Series Bankruptcy Judges Division brochure on "Bankruptcy Basics" prepared by the Administrative Office of the United States Courts, June 2000)

Chapter 12 of the Bankruptcy Code was enacted by Congress in 1986, specifically to meet the needs of financially distressed family farmers. The primary purpose of this legislation was to give family farmers facing bankruptcy a chance to reorganize their debts and keep their farms.

Background

In tailoring chapter 12 to meet the economic realities of family farming, this law has eliminated many of the barriers that family farmers had faced when seeking to reorganize successfully under either chapter 11 or 13 of the Bankruptcy Code. For example, chapter 12 is more streamlined, less complicated, and less expensive than chapter 11, which is better suited to the large corporate reorganization. In addition, few family farmers find chapter 13 to be advantageous, because it was designed for wage earners who have smaller debts than those facing family farmers. In chapter 12, Congress sought to combine the features of the Bankruptcy Code which can provide a framework for successful family farm reorganizations. At the time of the enactment of chapter 12, Congress could not be sure whether chapter 12 relief for the family farmer would be required indefinitely. Accordingly, the law (which first provided that no chapter 12 cases could be filed after September 30, 1993) currently provides that no cases may be filed under chapter 12 after July 1, 2000. As of June 30, 2000, legislation is pending in Congress to extend that deadline.

The Bankruptcy Code provides that only a family farmer with "regular annual income" may file a petition for relief under chapter 12. 11 U.S.C. §§ 101(18), 109(f). The purpose of this requirement is to ensure that the debtor's annual income is sufficiently stable and regular to permit the debtor to make payments under a chapter 12 plan. Allowance is made under chapter 12, however, for situations in which family farmers may have income that is seasonal in nature. Relief under this chapter is voluntary; thus, only the debtor may file a petition under chapter 12.

Under the Bankruptcy Code, those eligible to file as "family farmers" fall into two categories: (1) an individual or individual and spouse and (2) a corporation or partnership. Those falling into the first category must meet each of the following four criteria as of the date the petition is filed in order to qualify for relief under chapter 12.

1. More than one-half of the outstanding stock or equity in the corporation or partnership must be owned by one family or by one family and its relatives.

2. The family or the family and its relatives must conduct the farming operation.

3. More than 80% of the value of the corporate or partnership assets must be related to the farming operation.

4. The total indebtedness of the corporation or partnership must not exceed $1.5 million.

5. Not less than 80% of the corporation's or partnership's total debts which are fixed in amount must come from the farming operation owned or operated by

6. If the corporation has issued stock, the stock cannot be publicly traded.

What Bankruptcy Can and Cannot Do

Bankruptcy may make it possible for financially distressed individuals to:

1. Discharge liability for most or all of their debts and get a fresh start. When the debt is discharged, the debtor has no further legal obligation to pay the debt.

2. Stop foreclosure actions on their home and allow them an opportunity to catch up on missed payments.

3. Prevent repossession of a car or other property, or force the creditor to return property even after it has been repossessed.

4. Stop wage garnishment and other debt collection harassment, and give the individual some breathing room.

5. Restore or prevent termination of utility service.

6. Lower the monthly payments on debts, including secured debts such as car loans.

7. Allow debtors an opportunity to challenge the claims of certain creditors who have committed fraud or who are otherwise seeking to collect more than they are legally entitled to.

8. Bankruptcy, however, cannot cure every financial problem. It is usually not possible to:

9. Eliminate certain rights of secured creditors. Although a debtor can force secured creditors to take payments over time in the bankruptcy process, a debtor generally cannot keep the collateral unless the debtor continues to pay the debt.

Discharge types of debts singled out by the federal bankruptcy statutes for special treatment, such as child support, alimony, some student loans, certain court ordered payments, criminal fines, and some taxes.

Protect all cosigners on their debts. If relative or friend co-signed a loan which the debtor discharged in bankruptcy, the cosigner may still be obligated to repay the loan.

Discharge debts that are incurred after bankruptcy has been filed.

Bankruptcy's Effect on Your Credit

By federal law, a bankruptcy can remain part of a debtor's credit history for 10 years. Whether or not the debtor will be granted credit in the future is unpredictable. In some cases it may actually be easier to obtain future credit, because new creditors may feel that since the old obligations have been discharged, they will be first in line. The also recognize that the debtor cannot again file bankruptcy for at least the next six years.

Debtors have the option after bankruptcy of voluntarily paying some creditors, such as a doctor or hospital, with whom they wish to maintain credit. The payments are voluntary and do not reaffirm the past obligation.

About credit counseling agencies
11 U.S.C. § 342(b)(1)(B)

The following information is taken verbatim from the web site of the Federal Trade Commission. www.ftc.gov

Credit Counseling
If you're not disciplined enough to create a workable budget and stick to it, can't work out a repayment plan with your creditors, or can't keep track of mounting bills, consider contacting a credit counseling organization. Many credit counseling organizations are nonprofit and work with you to solve your financial problems. But be aware that, just because an organization says it's "nonprofit," there's no guarantee that its services are free, affordable, or even legitimate. In fact, some credit counseling organizations

charge high fees, which may be hidden, or urge consumers to make "voluntary" contributions that can cause more debt. Most credit counselors offer services through local offices, the Internet, or on the telephone. If possible, find an organization that offers in-person counseling. Many universities, military bases, credit unions, housing authorities, and branches of the U.S. Cooperative Extension Service operate nonprofit credit counseling programs. Your financial institution, local consumer protection agency, and friends and family also may be good sources of information and referrals.

Reputable credit counseling organizations can advise you on managing your money and debts, help you develop a budget, and offer free educational materials and workshops. Their counselors are certified and trained in the areas of consumer credit, money and debt management, and budgeting. Counselors discuss your entire financial situation with you, and help you develop a personalized plan to solve your money problems. An initial counseling session typically lasts an hour, with an offer of follow-up sessions.

Debt Management Plans:
If your financial problems stem from too much debt or your inability to repay your debts, a credit counseling agency may recommend that you enroll in a debt management plan (DMP). A DMP alone is not credit counseling, and DMPs are not for everyone. You should sign up for one of these plans only after a certified credit counselor has spent time thoroughly reviewing your financial situation, and has offered you customized advice on managing your money. Even if a DMP is appropriate for you, a reputable credit counseling organization still can help you create a budget and teach you money management skills.

In a DMP, you deposit money each month with the credit counseling organization, which uses your deposits to pay your unsecured debts, like your credit card bills, student loans, and medical bills, according to a payment schedule the counselor develops with you and your creditors. Your creditors may agree to lower your interest rates or waive certain fees, but check with all your creditors to be sure they offer the concessions that a credit counseling organization describes to you. A successful DMP requires you to make regular, timely payments, and could take 48 months or more to complete. Ask the credit counselor to estimate how long it will take for you to complete the plan. You may have to agree not to apply for — or use — any additional credit while you're participating in the plan.

DISCLOSURE #3

FULL DISCLOSURE & ACCURACY PURSUANT TO 11 U.S.C. § 527(a)(2)

If you file bankruptcy –

A. The information that you provide to your attorney, the bankruptcy trustee, and the court in the course of your bankruptcy, both before and after you file your bankruptcy petition, must be complete, accurate and truthful.

B. All of your assets (everything you own that has value, such as real estate, personal items, vehicles, money, etc.) and all of your liabilities (all of your debts) are required to be completely and accurately disclosed in the documents filed to start your case, and the replacement value of each asset must be stated in those documents where requested after reasonable inquiry to establish their value. The value should be your best understanding of how much it would cost you to replace the item in the same or similar condition.

C. You must provide your attorney with a monthly budget, including your current monthly income, all of your regular expenses, and the amount of your income that is left over after deduction of expenses. In listing your income and expenses, try to avoid guessing or estimating, and do your best effort to be accurate and truthful.

For income, you are required to provide information about all sources of your income, including your employment, any government assistance you may receive, social security, pension or other retirement income, income from side jobs, investment income, and similar sources.

D. The information that you provide to your bankruptcy attorney, the bankruptcy trustee, or the bankruptcy judge may be audited and will be available for inspection by the office of the United States Trustee, which is a branch of the U.S. Department of Justice.

If you fail to honestly and fully provide information about your property, income, expenses, and other financial circumstances, your case could be dismissed, and you could be subject to criminal sanctions.

DISCLOSURE # 4

INSTRUCTIONS REQUIRED TO BE PROVIDED TO THE DEBTOR PURSUANT TO 11 U.S.C. § 527(c)

According to Code § 527(c), the following information is required to be provided to a bankruptcy client only if the attorney (or other "debt relief agency") does not provide it. Since in the usual case the debtor cannot be presumed to have the analytical skills necessary to successfully handle this information, it is expected that in the ordinary case the lawyer or other bankruptcy professional handling the case will do the calculations required by this disclosure, it is not necessary that these instructions be provided to the debtor.

Instructions for providing the required information

1. How to place a value on your property

11 U.S.C. § 506(a): Fair Valuation of Collateral.

The value of your personal property that is collateral for debt (a debt where the creditor could repossess the item if you stop making payments, such as a car, furniture or computer equipment being purchased on installment) is determined based on the replacement value of such property as of the filing date of the bankruptcy case without deduction for selling or marketing costs.

If the item was acquired for personal, family, or household purposes, replacement value is the price a retail merchant would charge for an item of that kind, considering the age and condition of the property at the time its value is determined.

So, the value of the car, the furniture, the computer or anything else that you won't own until it's paid off, is not what you paid for it, and it is not what you could sell it for at the flea-market. The value is what you would have to pay a retail store selling similar items in a similar age and condition.

Most retail stores do not sell used items. However, there are usually stores in the are selling used furniture, musical instruments, cars, and similar products. You might be able to provide a good estimate of the value of one or your items by inquiring at such a store. If you can't find a store that sells similar items in similar condition, the next best source for an objective appraisal is probably eBay or a similar online market.

2. How to determine current monthly income

To arrive at your current monthly income, you do the following:

a.   Total up all of your income for the last 6 months (and if your spouse is filing bankruptcy, his or her income as well).

Include the contributions from any member of the household who is contributing regularly to the household expenses.

Income includes:

1.   Wages and salaries
2.   Money earned from side jobs
3.   Investment income
4.   Interest income
5.   Income for self-employed individuals

Income does not include:

1.   Benefits received under the Social Security Act;
2.   Payments to victims of war crimes or crimes against humanity on account of their status as victims of such crimes; and
3.   Payments to victims of international terrorism (as defined in section 2331 of Title 18) or domestic terrorism (as defined in section 2331 of Title 18) on account of their status as victims of such terrorism.

b.   Divide this figure by 6 to arrive at an average monthly income.

3. How to figure your necessary living expenses

Go through the same exercise for your expenses. Total up all expenses for the last 6 months, then divide by 6 to obtain a monthly average. Expenses include all of your reasonably necessary costs of living, such as rent or mortgage, utilities, food, transportation, etc.

Do not include in your expenses payments for credit cards, repayments of personal loans, delinquent medical bills, taxes, store charge accounts, business debts, or other non-regular expenses not included as necessary living expenses.

4. How to calculate your disposable income, if any.

If your average monthly income exceeds your reasonably necessary living expenses, subtract expenses from income; the surplus is your disposable income.

5. How to list your creditors (your debts)

For each person or entity (such as credit card, store, medical bill, IRS, mortgage, and etc.) for which you owe money, provide the following information:

1.   Name and address of the creditor
2.   The account number (if any)
3.   The amount currently owed
4.   The amount of the regular monthly payment (if any)
5.   When was the debt created (if a credit card, give a range)?
6.   Was the debt -
        - financing of a purchase (such as a home, car, furniture, etc.), or
        - a loan or debt for which you put up an item as collateral

7.   If either part of question 6 is yes, describe the item purchased

8.   What was the original retail price of the item?

9.   What is it's current value?

10.   Are you current with the monthly payments?

11.   If the answer to 10 is no, has the claim been turned over to a collection agency or lawyer?

12.   If 11 is yes, provide the name and address of the collection agency or lawyer.

13.   Has the creditor sued you or obtained a judgment against you?

14.   If 13 is yes, provide the name of the plaintiff, the case number, the court and court location, and the amount of the judgment.

6. How to determine which of your assets are exempt

Exempt assets are assets that the bankruptcy trustee is not allowed to take away from you to pay debts. Most kinds of property owned by typical people who file bankruptcy are exempt, meaning you don't lose them if you file bankruptcy. But whether an item is exempt or not depends not only on what category of property it is, but also the value of your equity in the property (how much of the item do you own, over and above any balance owed on it). The permissible exemptions usually have dollar limits to the amount of equity you can claim as exempt.

In order to identify which of your assets are exempt, you must know the exemptions allowed in your particular state, or whether your state uses the federal exemptions. Your attorney will review all of your assets with you after you have completed your worksheet to be certain that they are all exempt. The exemptions for Ohio can be found in Ohio Revised Code Section 2329.66.

DISCLOSURE # 5

FRAUD & CONCEALMENT PROHIBITED PURSUANT TO 11 U.S.C. § 342(b)(2)(A) and (B)

Debtor's Duties in Bankruptcy

If you decide to file bankruptcy, it is important that you understand the following:

1.   Some or all of the information you provide in connection with your bankruptcy will be filed with the bankruptcy court on forms or documents that you will be required to sign and declare as true under penalty of perjury.

2.   A person who knowingly and fraudulently conceals assets or makes a false oath or statement under penalty of perjury in connection with a bankruptcy case shall be subject to fine, imprisonment, or both.
11 U.S.C. § 342(b)(2)(A)

3.   All information you provide in connection with your bankruptcy case is subject to examination by the Attorney General.
11 U.S.C. § 342(b)(2)(B)